MCR

Compass Point
Phonics Readers

Where Is Your Home?

by Cindy Chapman

Reading Consultant: Wiley Blevins, M.A.
Phonics/Early Reading Specialist

COMPASS POINT BOOKS
Minneapolis, Minnesota

Compass Point Books
3109 West 50th Street, #115
Minneapolis, MN 55410

Visit Compass Point Books on the Internet at *www.compasspointbooks.com*
or e-mail your request to *custserv@compasspointbooks.com*

Photographs ©: Cover and p. 1 (left): The Image Finders, Inc./Jeff Greenberg, Cover and p.1
(right): Folio, Inc./Walter Bibikow, p. 6: Corbis/Will & Deni McIntyre, p. 7: Corbis/Ron Watts,
p. 8: Bruce Coleman, Inc./Guido Cozzi, p. 9: Corbis, p. 10: Corbis, p. 11: Index Stock Imagery/
Lynn M. Stone, p. 12 top left: Folio, Inc./Walter Bibikow, p. 12 bottom right: Index Stock
Imagery/Todd Powell, p. 12 top right: Index Stock Imagery/Chris Minerva

Editorial Development: Alice Dickstein, Alice Boynton
Photo Researcher: Wanda Winch
Design/Page Production: Silver Editions, Inc.

Library of Congress Cataloging-in-Publication Data
Chapman, Cindy.
  Where is your home? / by Cindy Chapman.
    p. cm. — (Compass Point phonics readers)
Includes bibliographical references and index.
Summary: Discusses different places to live, a city, a town, and the
country, in an easy-to-read text that incorporates phonics instruction
and rebuses.
  ISBN 0-7565-0532-1 (hardcover : alk. paper)
  1. Home—Juvenile literature. 2. City and town life—Juvenile
literature. 3. Country life—Juvenile literature. 4. Reading—Phonetic
method—Juvenile literature. [1. Home. 2. City and town life. 3. Country
life. 4. Rebuses. 5. Reading—Phonetic method.] I. Title. II. Series.
  HQ503C43 2003
  307.3'362—dc21   2003006377

Table of Contents

Dear Parent or Caregiver,

Welcome to Compass Point Phonics Readers, books of information for young children. Each book concentrates on specific phonic sounds and words commonly found in beginning reading materials. Featuring eye-catching photographs, every book explores a single science or social studies concept that is sure to grab a child's interest.

So snuggle up with your child, and let's begin. Start by reading aloud the Mother Goose nursery rhyme on the next page. As you read, stress the words in dark type. These are the words that contain the phonic sounds featured in this book. After several readings, pause before the rhyming words, and let your child chime in.

Now let's read *Where Is Your Home?* If your child is a beginning reader, have him or her first read it silently. Then ask your child to read it aloud. For children who are not yet reading, read the book aloud as you run your finger under the words. Ask your child to imitate, or "echo," what he or she has just heard.

Discussing the book's content with your child:
Explain to your child that a neighborhood is a small part of a larger community in which people live. People in neighborhoods share parks, schools, fire stations, and libraries.

At the back of the book is a fun Tic-Tac-Toe game. Your child will take pride in demonstrating his or her mastery of the phonic sounds and the high-frequency words.

Enjoy Compass Point Phonics Readers and watch your child read and learn!

Elsie Marley

Elsie Marley has grown so **fine,**
She won't get up to serve the **swine,**
But lies in bed till eight or **nine,**
And surely she does take her **time.**

Pete lives in a city.
It is a big place.
It has big buildings.
It has lots of people.

Pete rides in buses and cabs.
Pete takes trips with his class to
see dinosaur bones.
Pete likes the city.

Rosa lives in a town.
It has smaller  buildings.
It has lots of homes.

Rosa can play in her backyard.
Rosa can skate at an ice rink.
She makes a cake for a bake sale.
Rosa likes the town.

Pam lives in the country.
It has farms.
It has lakes and ponds to swim in.
Pam can see for miles!

Pam can pet a rabbit.
She helps plant crops.
She likes the [deer]  and mules.
Pam likes the country.

Look at these places.
Where is your home?

Word List

Final e

a_e
bake
cake
lakes
makes
place(s)
sale
skate
takes

e_e
Pete
these

i_e
ice
likes
miles
rides

o_e
bones
home(s)

u_e
mules

Digraph th
these
with

High-Frequency
her
play
smaller

Social Studies
city
country
people
town

Tic-Tac-Toe

Game 1

bake	with	home
likes	race	takes
note	rides	lakes

How to Play

- Players take turns reading aloud a word and then covering it with a game piece.
- The first player to cover 3 words in a row down, across, or on the diagonal wins.
- After playing Game 1, the players can go to Game 2.

Game 2

ice	cake	these
place	miles	bones
skate	mule	makes

Read More

Bullard, Lisa. *My Home: Walls, Floors, Ceilings, and Doors.* Minneapolis, Minn.: Picture Window Books, 2003.

Roop, Peter, and Connie Roop. *A Town.* Walk Around Series. Des Plaines, Ill.: Heinemann Library, 1999.

Saunders-Smith, Gail. *Communities.* Mankato, Minn.: Capstone Press, 1998.

Schaefer, Lola M. *Apartment.* A Home for Me Series. Chicago, Ill.: Heinemann Library, 2002.

Index